Unsolved!

MYSTERIES OF WATER MONSTERS

Kathryn Walker

based on original text by Brian Innes

Crabtree Publishing Company

www.crabtreebooks.com

Crabtree Publishing Company

www.crabtreebooks.com

Author: Kathryn Walker
  based on original text by Brian Innes
Project editor: Kathryn Walker
Picture researcher: Rachel Tisdale
Managing editor: Miranda Smith
Art director: Jeni Child
Design manager: David Poole
Editorial director: Lindsey Lowe
Children's publisher: Anne O'Daly
Editor: Molly Aloian
Proofreaders: Adrianna Morganelli, Crystal Sikkens
Project coordinator: Robert Walker
Production coordinator: Katherine Kantor
Prepress technician: Katherine Kantor

This edition published in 2009 by
Crabtree Publishing Company

The Brown Reference Group plc
First Floor
9-17 St. Albans Place
London N1 0NX
www.brownreference.com

Copyright © 2008 The Brown Reference Group plc

Photographs:
Fortean Picture Library: p. 6–7,
  8, 10, 11, 15, 16, 17, 20, 24, 25,
  26–27, 28 (top)
Mary Evans Picture Library: p. 4–5, 21
Shutterstock: Albert Barr: p. 9;
  Chris Harvey: p. 13 (bottom right);
  Adrian T. Jones: p. 13 (top);
  Mary Lane: p. 18–19;
  RM: p. 22–23;
  Wheatley: p. 29
Topfoto: Charles Walker: cover
Wikipedia Commons: Ballista: p. 30;
  Harper's Weekly: p. 28 (bottom);
  Adrian Pingstone: p. 14

Every effort has been made to trace the
owners of copyrighted material.

Library and Archives Canada Cataloguing in Publication

Walker, Kathryn, 1957-
    Mysteries of water monsters / Kathryn Walker based on original
text by Brian Innes.

(Unsolved!)
Includes index.
ISBN 978-0-7787-4146-6 (bound).--ISBN 978-0-7787-4159-6 (pbk.)

    1. Sea monsters--Juvenile literature. 2. Marine animals--Juvenile
literature. I. Innes, Brian II. Title. III. Series: Unsolved!
(St. Catharines, Ont.)

QL122.2.W34 2008   j001.944   C2008-904329-4

Library of Congress Cataloging-in-Publication Data

Walker, Kathryn, 1957-
    Mysteries of water monsters / Kathryn Walker based on original text by Brian Innes.
      p. cm. -- (Unsolved!)
    Includes index.
    ISBN-13: 978-0-7787-4159-6 (pbk. : alk. paper)
    ISBN-10: 0-7787-4159-1 (pbk. : alk. paper)
    ISBN-13: 978-0-7787-4146-6 (reinforced library binding : alk. paper)
    ISBN-10: 0-7787-4146-X (reinforced library binding : alk. paper)
    1. Marine animals--Juvenile literature. 2. Sea monsters--Juvenile literature. I. Innes,
Brian Water monsters. II. Title.

QL122.2W35 2009
001.944--dc22
                                                    2008030107

Crabtree Publishing Company

www.crabtreebooks.com   1-800-387-7650

Published in Canada
Crabtree Publishing
616 Welland Ave.
St. Catharines, ON
L2M 5V6

Published in the United States
Crabtree Publishing
PMB16A
350 Fifth Ave., Suite 3308
New York, NY 10118

Contents

Monster Attack!

...In the late 1700s, a terrifying attack by a sea monster was reported.

Jean-Magnus Dens was captain of a Danish ship. He had a frightening story to tell. His ship had been sailing off the west coast of Africa. The waters were calm, so the captain told some men to clean the outside of the ship. They were lowered over the side to do so.

Suddenly, a monster with huge tentacles rose out of the sea. It threw a tentacle around two of the men and pulled them into the water. Then another giant tentacle grabbed a third sailor. The crew rescued the man by chopping it off. The monster sank out of sight.

The piece of **tentacle** was about 25 feet (7.5 m) long. The captain guessed that the whole tentacle had been 40 feet (12 m) long.

How Strange...

In 1861, the crew of a French ship found the body of a huge sea creature. It had many tentacles that were covered with **suckers**.

At that time, some people did not believe such a creature existed. Today we know it does. It is called the giant squid.

>> **tentacle** — A long, flexible, arm-like part of an animal used for feeling or grasping

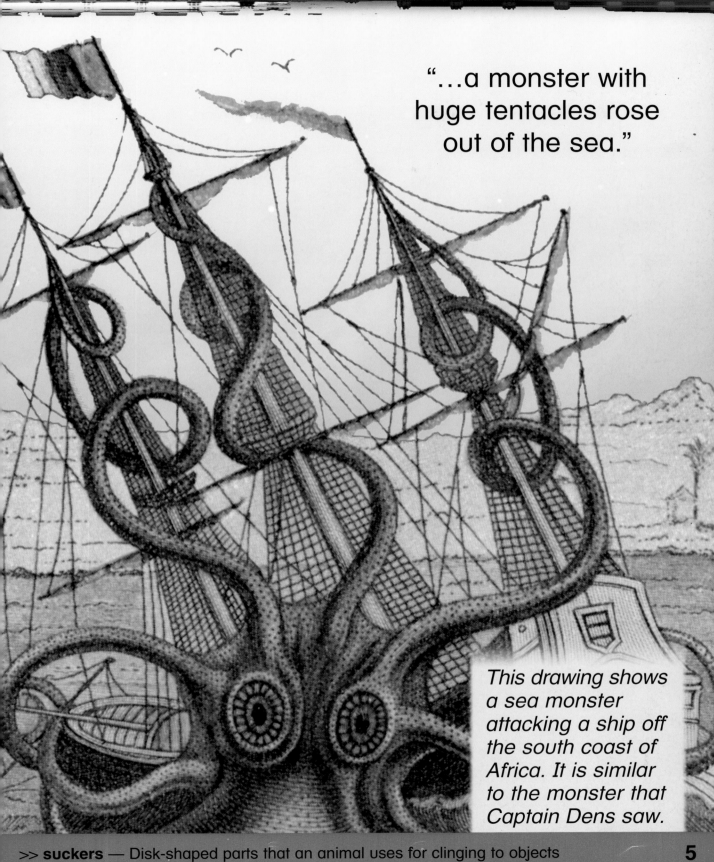

"...a monster with huge tentacles rose out of the sea."

This drawing shows a sea monster attacking a ship off the south coast of Africa. It is similar to the monster that Captain Dens saw.

Sea Monsters

...Stories of monsters living in the oceans come from all over the world.

For centuries, people have told tales of giant creatures from the sea. A sea monster named **Leviathan** is mentioned five times in the Bible. It is described as a "crooked serpent" and "the dragon that is in the sea."

Olaus Magnus lived in Sweden more than 450 years ago. He collected many stories about Leviathan. Magnus described the creature as black with a **mane**. It ate calves and lambs. It would even drag men from their boats.

Sailors from Norway told tales of the Kraken. This enormous sea monster was said to attack ships and eat the sailors. It was described as having huge tentacles. Many people today think that the Kraken may have been a giant squid. These creatures live in the deep sea and are known to grow up to 59 feet (18 m) long.

How Strange...

- A giant squid has eight arms and two tentacles.

- Its eyes are the largest of any known animal. They measure up to 11 inches (28 cm) across.

- The giant squid fights with whales. It does this by wrapping its tentacles around them.

>> **Leviathan** — Describes anything of immense size and power

"This enormous sea monster was said
to attack ships and eat the sailors."

This picture of a sea monster attack is taken from Olaus Magnus' book The History of the Northern Peoples. It was printed in 1555.

Some sea monsters are said to look like giant snakes. These are known as sea serpents.

Morgawr

For many years, people have reported seeing a sea serpent in the Falmouth Bay area of Cornwall, England. The monster is known as "Morgawr," which is an old Cornish word meaning "sea giant."

In 1976, a woman calling herself "Mary F." produced photographs of Morgawr. She said that the beast she saw had humps on its back. Its neck was long, with a small, snake-like head.

The photographs looked real. But Mary F. would not give her full name and address. She would not let people examine the pictures. Some people wondered if this was because they were fakes.

How Strange...

Some people believe that Morgawr could be a type of long-necked seal.

This photograph of Morgawr was taken by Mary F. in 1976.

"Its neck was long, with a small, snake-like head."

>> **humpback** — A crooked back that appears hunched

This is a picture of Chesapeake Bay, Maryland. "Chessie" the sea serpent has often been seen there.

Chessie

Another famous sea serpent lives on the other side of the Atlantic Ocean. For many years, people have seen the creature in Chesapeake Bay, Maryland. Local people call it "Chessie."

Robert and Karen Frew had a house on Kent Island in Chesapeake Bay. On May 21, 1982, they spotted Chessie. Robert grabbed his video camera and filmed it from a bedroom window. Chessie was about 35 feet (10.5 m) long and 1 foot (30 cm) wide, with a **humpback**.

Experts watched the Frews' videotape, but the pictures were **blurred**. They were not able to decide what the creature could be.

> "For many years, people have seen the creature in Chesapeake Bay."

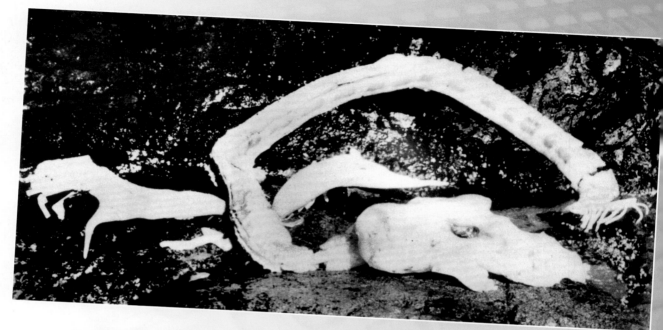

"Caddy"

The Pacific Coast, near Vancouver, in Canada, is also home to a sea monster. This monster is named "Caddy" because it has often been spotted in Cadboro Bay. It is a long, snake-like creature with flippers.

There were many sightings of Caddy in the early 1930s. On October 21, 1933, the ship Santa Lucia was close to Cadboro Bay. The **first officer** reported seeing a "great eel-like monster." He said it was about 90 feet (27 m) long with humps.

In 1936, a strange skeleton was found on the coast near Vancouver. People wondered if it was Caddy. But the sightings did not stop.

This picture shows an animal's remains found at Camp Fircom, British Columbia, in 1936. Was this Caddy or the skeleton of some other creature? Or could the picture have been a **hoax**?

>> **first officer** — The officer on a ship who is second only to the captain

Monster Hoax

Robert Le Serrec was a French photographer. In 1964, Le Serrec said that he had taken some photographs of a sea monster off the coast of Queensland, Australia. This creature was shaped like a giant tadpole. He said it had been about 75–80 feet (23–24 m) long.

At first, Le Serrec's pictures caused great excitement. But then it was reported that he had told people he had a plan for making a lot of money. He had said that his plan had something to do with a sea serpent.

Today, most people believe that Le Serrec's pictures were a hoax.

Robert Le Serrec astonished the world with this photograph. It appeared to show a sea monster.

"Le Serrec said that he had taken some photographs of a sea monster… shaped like a giant tadpole."

The Loch Ness Monster

..."Nessie" is probably the most famous water monster in the world.

Loch Ness is a long, narrow lake in the Highlands of Scotland. It is less than 1 mile (1.6 km) wide, but up to 788 feet (240 m) deep. We know that a monster was seen in the lake more than 1,400 years ago.

In the year 565, a **holy** man named St. Columba went to Scotland. At Loch Ness, he saw the monster. It was coming to attack a man who was swimming nearby. St. Columba commanded the monster to go back. At the sound of his voice, the monster turned away.

Since then, there have been many sightings of the Loch Ness monster. In Scotland, it became known as "Niseag." This is a **Scottish Gaelic** word. Its English name is "Nessie."

How Strange...

Nessie is said to have a long, thin neck. Its head looks small compared to its large body.

Some people have reported that the monster has a face like a camel.

>> **holy** — Dedicated to the service of God

Above is a picture of Loch Ness at sunset. On the right is an artist's idea of what the Loch Ness monster looks like.

In the 1930s, a new road was built along the north shore of Loch Ness. This made it easier for people to get to the lake. Soon, Nessie was in the news.

More Sightings

On July 22, 1933, George Spicer and his wife were driving by the lake. They saw a huge, black beast cross the road. George Spicer said it had a long neck, "a little thicker than an elephant's trunk."

In 1934, Arthur Grant said he nearly hit the monster while riding his motorbike. He said it had a long neck with a small head. The body was large, with flippers and a tail. Grant thought it was about 20 feet (6 m) long. This monster sounds like a **plesiosaur**. But scientists believe that this animal died out 65 million years ago.

"...it had a long neck with a small head. The body was large, with flippers and a tail."

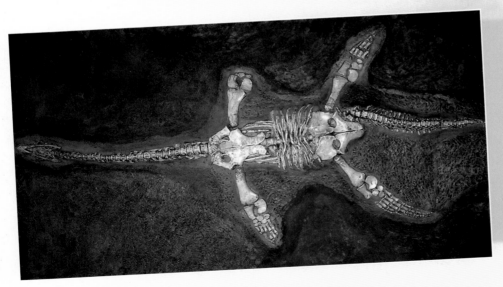

This picture shows a copy of a plesiosaur skeleton. The real skeleton was found in Somerset, England, in 2002.

>> **plesiosaur** — A large marine reptile with flippers that lived 220 million years ago

This is the picture of Nessie that Robert Wilson produced in 1934. For years, people believed it was the best photograph ever taken of the monster.

Photographs and Film

In November 1933, Hugh Gray claimed he had taken the first photograph of Nessie. The picture was very blurred, but it was printed in newspapers all over the world.

Other photographs followed. Some were proved to be hoaxes. Some looked as if they could be pictures of logs. It is difficult to be sure exactly what the others show.

In 2007, Gordon Holmes claimed he had videotaped Nessie. The video seems to be real. But some people think it could show a known animal, such as an otter or a seal.

How Strange...

One of the most famous photos of Nessie was taken by Colonel Robert Wilson in 1934. Sixty years later, a model-maker admitted that the photo was a fake. He said he had made the model of Nessie using a toy **submarine**!

In 1968, a team of scientists set up a sonar scanner at Loch Ness. This is a machine that picks up sounds made by moving objects. On August 28, the sonar scanner recorded something moving in the lake.

A large object traveled up from the bottom of the lake. Then it turned and dove deep. At the same time, there were sounds made by a second object. Scientists thought that the objects were moving too fast to be **schools** of fish.

Jennifer Bruce took this photograph in 1982. It is part of a much bigger photograph. She said she did not notice the monster's head when she was taking it.

The Flipper Photo

Dr. Robert Rines from Massachusetts, in the United States, decided to investigate. In 1972, he led a team that took underwater photographs in Loch Ness. The lake was dark and the pictures were not clear. But they seemed to show the flipper of a large animal.

In 1975, the team took more photographs. The pictures showed something like the head and neck of a creature. Some people thought this proved there were large animals in Loch Ness.

>> **schools** — Large groups of fish or whales swimming together

More Searches

In 1987, 24 motorboats swept across the lake to try to find the monster. This was known as "Operation Deepscan." Each boat carried sonar equipment. The sonar **detected** three objects moving in the lake. They were bigger than sharks, but smaller than whales.

Since then, other groups have used special equipment to search the lake. Some of them have also detected objects moving in the water. But nothing new has been discovered.

In 2003, a team of experts used sonar to search the lake. They swept the lake from top to bottom. They could find no sign of any large animal living in Loch Ness.

"The sonar detected three objects moving in the lake."

This photograph shows a fleet of motorboats sweeping across Loch Ness in 1987. The boats were part of Operation Deepscan, an attempt to solve the mystery of the lake.

Lakes of North America

..Loch Ness is not the only lake with a monster.

Lake Champlain lies between New York State and Vermont. This long lake is home to one of North America's most famous water monsters. The monster is known as "Champ."

The lake is named for French explorer Samuel de Champlain. Stories say that he spotted a monster here in 1609. But the first recorded report of Champ was in 1819. This was when a boatman said he had seen a huge creature with a long neck. Champ has been seen many times since then.

In July 1883, Captain Nathan H. Mooney gave a very clear **description** of Champ. He said he had watched an enormous, snake-like monster rise out of the water. Captain Mooney said that its body was about 25–30 feet (8–9 m) long. Its neck was "like a goose when about to take flight."

>> **description** — An account of something

How Strange...

 In 1977, Mrs. Sandra Mansi took a photograph of Champ. Many people think the photograph looks real.

This photo showed a dark body with a long neck. Mrs. Mansi thought the beast looked like a dinosaur.

"...a boatman said he had seen a huge creature with a long neck."

This picture shows the Sun setting at Lake Champlain. The lake is 109 miles (175 km) long. It is a huge playground for the water monster "Champ."

Snake in the Lake

Ogopogo is another famous North American monster. It is said to live in Lake Okanagan, in British Columbia, Canada. Native Americans called it Naitaka. This means "snake of the water."

Many people claim they have seen Ogopogo. In 1952, a woman said she had seen the monster very clearly. It had a head like a cow or a horse. Along its back were ragged edges, like a saw. "It was a wonderful sight," she said.

People say they have captured Ogopogo in photographs and on film. The most interesting piece of film was shot by Art Folden in 1968. It shows a creature about 60 feet (18 m) long moving very fast and leaving a clear **wake**.

This picture of Ogopogo comes from a postcard. Many people say they have seen a huge, snake-like monster like this in Lake Okanagan.

" Along its back were ragged edges, like a saw. 'It was a wonderful sight,' she said."

>> **wake** — A track of waves left by something moving through water

Ponik

Monsters are said to live in many other Canadian lakes. Lake Pohénégamook in Quebec has one named "Ponik." Some people have seen a giant fish there. Others have reported that Ponik is a snake-like creature.

Memphrémagog's Monster

Lake Memphrémagog lies on the **border** between Canada and the state of Maine. Native Americans were afraid to swim there. They believed that a monster lived in the lake.

Today, people still report seeing a monster in the lake. Some say it is like a whale. Others claim to have seen a long, humped animal.

How Strange...

Experts believe that many of the monsters seen in Canadian lakes are really giant sturgeons. These huge fish are known to grow up to 12 feet (3.5 m) long.

Some people think that the lake monsters could be a type of dinosaur.

This strange-looking creature is a type of fish that is called a sturgeon. Some people think that giant sturgeons are sometimes mistaken for water monsters.

>> **border** — A boundary or line that separates two countries or regions

Lakes Around the World

...Many countries have lakes where strange beasts are said to live.

Lake Nahuel Huapi lies in the Andes Mountains of southern Argentina. Its deep, blue waters hide South America's most famous monster. This beast is known as "Nahuelito."

Nahuelito seems to come to the surface only on calm summer days. First there is a sudden **swell** and a spray of water. Then Nahuelito appears.

People have given many different descriptions of Nahuelito. Some say they have seen a giant water snake with humps and fins. Others claim to have seen a creature that looks like a swan with a snake's head. Reports of Nahuelito's length also vary. Its length has been said to be anything from 15–150 feet (4.5–45 m).

>> **swell** — A bulge or rise in the water

How Strange...

In 1782, Juan Ignacio Molina wrote about a different type of South American lake monster. He said that the natives of Chile talked of a huge fish or dragon that ate people. They called it the "fox-serpent."

*This is the beautiful Lake Nahuel Huapi in Argentina. Could a monster **lurk** beneath this calm surface?*

On the other side of the world, people tell stories of a monster called "mokele-mbembe." This beast is said to live in the Likoula **swamp** region in the Republic of the Congo. This is a country in central Africa.

Killer Creature

The mokele-mbembe is a terrifying creature that can be the size of an elephant. It has a long neck and clawed feet. People say the mokele-mbembe attacks canoes and will kill anyone aboard.

In 1980 and 1981, scientist Roy Mackal set out to find the mokele-mbembe. His team of explorers searched the Likoula swamp, but they could not find any sign of it.

This picture shows a mokele-mbembe (right) with a hippo. People say that the monster does not like hippos and will fight or kill them.

>> **swamp** — Low land with trees and shrubs that is usually covered in water

The Water-Horse

Throughout Europe, there are many reports of a lake monster known as a "water-horse." This creature is often said to have a horse-like face.

There are tales of water-horses in Ireland, Scotland, Iceland, and Norway. One of the most famous water-horses lives in Lake Storsjön in Sweden.

Sightings of the Lake Storsjön monster go back hundreds of years. Some **witnesses** have said that the monster looks like a large eel. Others have described seeing a much bigger creature, sometimes with humps and a dog-like head.

The three monsters in this picture all look very different. But each one has been drawn from reports of the Lake Storsjön monster.

>> **witness** — Someone who has seen an event taking place and can describe what happened **25**

What Are They?

...Some reports of water monsters may be hoaxes or imagined. But what about the rest?

Reports of monsters have created a new word—**cryptozoologist**. "Crypto" means "hidden," and a zoologist is someone who studies animals. Cryptozoologists are people who study and search for unknown animals.

Dr. Bernard Heuvelmans was a cryptozoologist. He spent many years studying reports of sea monsters. Heuvelmans found he could divide them into nine different types of creatures.

The type of sea monster most often reported was the long-necked sea serpent. Another type was a creature that people said was shaped like a crocodile. Heuvelmans thought this might be an animal left over from the time when dinosaurs lived on Earth.

How Strange...

Heuvelmans thought that the long-necked sea serpent might be a type of giant sea lion.

Another group of sea monsters were ones with many humps. Heuvelmans thought that they might be an ancient type of whale.

>> **cryptozoologist** — Someone who studies animals that may or may not exist

"…cryptozoologists are people who study and search for unknown animals."

This picture shows the ancient reptile called a plesiosaur. Many people have said they have seen water monsters that look like plesiosaurs.

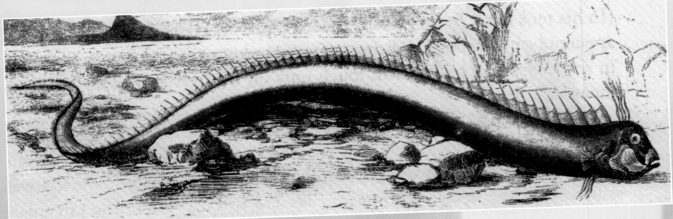

Survivors?

Cryptozoologists have suggested that the sea serpent might be a zeuglodon. This is an early type of whale. It is supposed to have died out about 35 million years ago, but maybe some have **survived**.

Many descriptions of water monsters sound like the plesiosaur (see page 27). This large water reptile lived at the same time as the dinosaurs. Plesiosaurs had long necks, small heads, and wide bodies. Some people wonder if a few are still living in lakes and oceans.

At the top is a picture of a sea serpent. Below it is a drawing of an oarfish. You can see why people mistake the oarfish for a monster.

>> **survived** — Continued to live after others in its group have died

Mistaken Identity

Some creatures we know about can easily be mistaken for water monsters. For example, oarfish have very long, ribbon-like bodies. They can be up to 41 feet (12.5 m) long and have red spikes down their backs. People who have seen an oarfish often think they have seen a monster.

The **basking shark** is one of the largest types of fish. It can also be mistaken for a water monster, particularly when only its fins are seen sticking out of the water.

Dead basking sharks often cause great excitement. Because of the way their body rots, their remains can look like those of sea monsters or even plesiosaurs.

"People who have seen an oarfish often think they have seen a monster."

This basking shark is lying on the floor of an aquarium. These huge fish can grow to be up to 40 feet (12 m) long.

What could water monsters be? People who do not believe they exist have many explanations. One is that the humps of a sea serpent are really a line of porpoises jumping out of the water.

Unknown Species?

Every year, thousands of new **species** of creatures are discovered. Maybe water monsters are simply animals we do not yet know about. People used to think that the giant squid was just a sea story. But in the 1870s, people discovered it really did exist.

Ancient Animals

Could water monsters be species that we think have died out, but are in fact still living? The coelacanth is a fish that scientists thought died out 65 million years ago. Then in 1938, some fishermen caught one. Since that time, others have been found. The coelacanth is alive and well!

For many years, scientists thought that this coelacanth had died out with the dinosaurs. Now we have proof that the fish still exists.

There are huge areas of the Earth that humans have not yet explored. Many are in the oceans. Who knows what might be living in deep waters?

>> **species** — Groups or types of animals or plants

Glossary

basking shark A very large shark that often floats near the surface of the ocean

blurred Unclear or hazy in appearance

border A boundary or line that separates two countries or regions

cryptozoologist Someone who studies animals that may or may not exist

description An account of something

detected Discovered that there was something

dinosaur A type of reptile that lived millions of years ago

first officer The officer on a ship who is second only to the captain

hoax A trick

holy Dedicated to the service of God

humpback A crooked back that appears hunched

Leviathan Describes anything of immense size and power

lurk To be hidden or move about quietly

mane Long hair that grows on the back of or around the neck of some animals

plesiosaur A large marine reptile with flippers that lived 220 million years ago

schools Large groups of fish or whales swimming together

Scottish Gaelic A language spoken in parts of northern Scotland

sea lion A large type of seal

species Groups or types of animals or plants

submarine A ship that travels underwater

suckers Disk-shaped parts that an animal uses for clinging to objects

survived Continued to live after others in its group have died

swamp Low land with trees and shrubs that is usually covered in water

swell A bulge or rise in the water

tentacle A long, flexible, arm-like part of an animal used for feeling or grasping

wake A track of waves left by something moving through water

witness Someone who has seen an event taking place and can describe what happened

Index

Further Reading

• DK Publishing. Myths and Monsters, "Secret Worlds" series. DK Children, 2003.

• Krensky, Stephen. Creatures from the Deep, "Monster Chronicles" series. Lerner Publications, 2007.

• Miller, Karen. Monsters and Water Beasts: Creatures of Fact or Fiction? Henry Holt and Co., 2007.

• Sievert, Terry. The Loch Ness Monster, "The Unexplained" series. Edge Books, 2004.

Printed in the U.S.A.